D0021277

This little holiday book belongs to

Amanda

I love you

MaryLynn

OVER THE RIVER

THROUGH THE WOODS

Over the River
and Through the Woods

Illustrated by
Mary Engelbreit

Andrews and McMeel
A Universal Press Syndicate Company
Kansas City

Over the River and Through the Woods copyright
© Mary Engelbreit Ink 1994. All rights reserved.
Printed in Singapore. No part of this book may be
used or reproduced in any manner whatsoever
without written permission except in the case of
reprints in the context of reviews. For information
write Andrews and McMeel, a Universal Press
Syndicate Company, 4900 Main Street, Kansas City,
Missouri 64112.

 is a registered trademark of Mary Engelbreit
Enterprises, Inc.

ISBN: 0-8362-4622-5

Over the River
and Through the Woods

Over the river
and through the woods,
there's a holiday mood in the air.

OVER THE RIVER

THROUGH THE WOODS

There's an anticipation
of Christmastime magic…

...and Yuletide excitement to share!

MERRILY · MERRILY

19·85
ME

MERRILY · MERRILY

A bright winter moon
lights a soft, solemn snowfall…

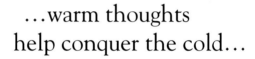

…warm thoughts
help conquer the cold…

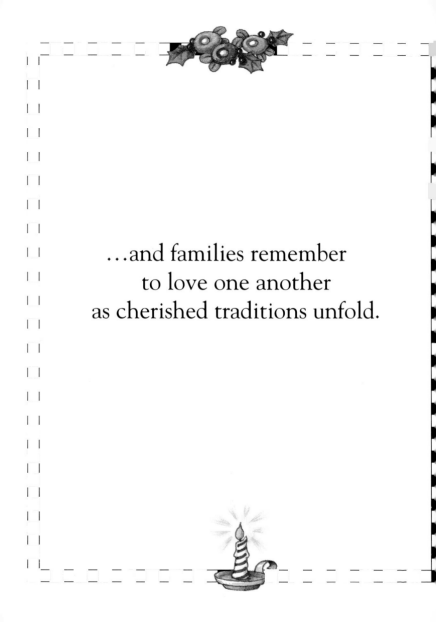

...and families remember
to love one another
as cherished traditions unfold.

Wintertime fantasies come to fruition
as sugarplums dance in the heads
of wide-eyed believers
who hang up their stockings,
then nestle down snug in their beds.

Merry
Christmas ♥

Treasured remembrances
tug at our heartstrings
bringing our past ever near…

BUT NOT ALONE AT CHRISTMASTIME
COMES HOLIDAY AND CHEER,
FOR ONE WHO LOVES A LITTLE
CHILD HAS   CHRISTMAS ALL
                    THE YEAR.

• FLORENCE EVELYN PRATT •

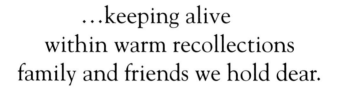

...keeping alive
within warm recollections
family and friends we hold dear.

REMEMBRANCE, LIKE A CANDLE····· BURNS BRIGHTEST AT CHRISTMAS TIME

The season surrounds us
with fond reminiscence…

...and all of the joy it imparts...

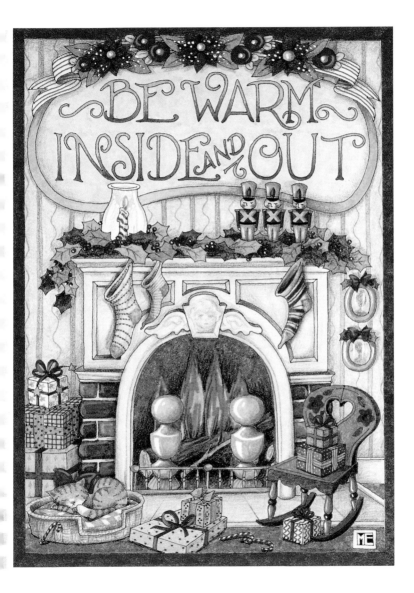

...as over the river
and through the woods,
we travel back home...
in our hearts.